...cy and
Dallas.

Precious Jesus
Loves You.

Stay Safe and Be
Blessed.

Hal O'

2020/Sept./21

Precious Jesus

I SAMUEL 15:2:2

OBEDIENCE IS THE KEY TO THE PRECIOUS HEART
OF JESUS. READ THE RED (THE WRITTEN WORD OF
JESUS) AND YOU WILL SURELY BE FED.

HAL O'

WESTBOW
PRESS®
A DIVISION OF THOMAS NELSON
& ZONDERVAN

Scripture taken from the Holy Bible, NEW INTERNATIONAL VERSION®. Copyright © 1973, 1978, 1984 by Biblica, Inc. All rights reserved worldwide. Used by permission. NEW INTERNATIONAL VERSION® and NIV® are registered trademarks of Biblica, Inc. Use of either trademark for the offering of goods or services requires the prior written consent of Biblica US, Inc.

WestBow Press books may be ordered through booksellers or by contacting:

WestBow Press
A Division of Thomas Nelson & Zondervan
1663 Liberty Drive
Bloomington, IN 47403
www.westbowpress.com
1 (866) 928-1240

Because of the dynamic nature of the Internet, any web addresses or links contained in this book may have changed since publication and may no longer be valid. The views expressed in this work are solely those of the author and do not necessarily reflect the views of the publisher, and the publisher hereby disclaims any responsibility for them.

Any people depicted in stock imagery provided by Thinkstock are models, and such images are being used for illustrative purposes only. Certain stock imagery © Thinkstock.

ISBN: 978-1-5127-2376-2 (sc)
ISBN: 978-1-5127-2375-5 (e)

Library of Congress Control Number: 2015920537

Print information available on the last page.

WestBow Press rev. date: 1/15/2016

CONTENTS

PUT JESUS FIRST

PUT JESUS FIRST, MAKE HIM A PART OF YOUR DAY.
PUT JESUS FIRST, WALK WITH HIM EVERY STEP OF THE WAY.

PUT JESUS FIRST, TALK WITH HIM EACH HOUR.
PUT JESUS FIRST, HE WILL FILL YOU WITH HIS POWER.

PUT JESUS FIRST, HE WILL TAKE AWAY ALL YOUR FEARS.
PUT JESUS FIRST, HE IS THE GOOD SHEPHERD THAT ALWAYS CARES.

PUT JESUS FIRST, THERE IS NO MOUNTAIN HE CAN NOT SCALE.
PUT JESUS FIRST, IN HIM THERE IS NO ROOM TO FAIL.

PUT JESUS FIRST, HE IS THE LIVING WATER.
PUT JESUS FIRST, HE GIVES LIFE NOW AND HEREAFTER.

PUT JESUS FIRST, HE IS THE RISEN SAVIOUR.
PUT JESUS FIRST, HE IS WORTHY OF ALL TO SAVOUR.

PUT JESUS FIRST, HE IS THE LORD OF ALL.
PUT JESUS FIRST, HE WILL ANSWER WHEN YOU CALL.

I WILL PUT YOU FIRST PRECIOUS JESUS. HELP ME PRECIOUS HOLY SPIRIT
TO PLACE MY HEAVENLY FATHER, MY LORD AND SAVIOUR JESUS CHRIST
AND YOU PRECIOUS SPIRIT FIRST PLACE IN MY LIFE. I ASK THIS IN THE
MOST PRECIOUS NAME OF JESUS. AMEN AND AMEN.

TAKE FIRST PLACE IN MY LIFE PRECIOUS JESUS

TAKE FIRST PLACE IN MY LIFE PRECIOUS JESUS,
HELP ME NOT TO FUSS, ONLY TO TRUST.

TAKE FIRST PLACE IN MY LIFE PRECIOUS JESUS,
HELP ME NOT TO FEAR, BECAUSE YOU ARE ALWAYS NEAR.

TAKE FIRST PLACE IN MY LIFE PRECIOUS JESUS,
HELP ME NOT TO BE ASHAMED, BUT TO BE PROUD OF YOUR HOLY NAME.

TAKE FIRST PLACE IN MY LIFE PRECIOUS JESUS,
HELP ME TO BRING GOOD NEWS ABOUT THE KING THAT WE CHOOSE.

TAKE FIRST PLACE IN MY LIFE PRECIOUS JESUS,
HELP ME TO REALIZE THAT YOU ARE THE ONLY WORTHY PRIZE.

TAKE FIRST PLACE IN MY LIFE PRECIOUS JESUS,
HELP ME TO SEE YOUR GOODNESS TOWARDS ME.

TAKE FIRST PLACE IN MY LIFE PRECIOUS JESUS,
HELP ME TO GIVE YOU PRAISE, FOR ME YOU DID RAISE.

MY LIFE IS YOURS PRECIOUS JESUS, PLEASE TAKE FIRST PLACE. I DECLARE
THIS IN YOUR PRECIOUS NAME JESUS. AMEN AND AMEN.

PRECIOUS LORD JESUS YOU HAVE FORBIDDEN ME

PRECIOUS LORD JESUS YOU HAVE FORBIDDEN ME TO GO ASTRAY.
PRECIOUS LORD JESUS YOU HAVE FORBIDDEN ME TO WALK MY OWN WAY.

PRECIOUS LORD JESUS YOU HAVE FORBIDDEN ME TO NEGLECT THE POOR.
PRECIOUS LORD JESUS YOU HAVE FORBIDDEN ME TO CLOSE THAT DOOR.

PRECIOUS LORD JESUS YOU HAVE FORBIDDEN ME TO DEPEND ON MY FELLOW MAN.
PRECIOUS LORD JESUS YOU HAVE FORBIDDEN ME BECAUSE THAT IS NOT YOUR PLAN.

PRECIOUS LORD JESUS YOU HAVE FORBIDDEN ME TO DO MY WILL.
PRECIOUS LORD JESUS YOU HAVE FORBIDDEN ME TO SIT AND BE STILL.

PRECIOUS LORD JESUS YOU HAVE FORBIDDEN ME TO LIVE ONLY FOR ME.
PRECIOUS LORD JESUS YOU HAVE FORBIDDEN ME TO BE BLIND AND NOT SEE.

PRECIOUS LORD JESUS YOU HAVE FORBIDDEN ME TO PASS THE BLAME.
PRECIOUS LORD JESUS YOU HAVE FORBIDDEN ME TO PLAY THAT GAME.

PRECIOUS LORD JESUS YOU HAVE FORBIDDEN ME TO LIVE IN FEAR.
PRECIOUS LORD JESUS YOU HAVE FORBIDDEN ME TO ACT LIKE I DO NOT CARE.

HEAVENLY FATHER I THANK YOU THAT THE FEW THINGS THAT YOU HAVE FORBIDDEN ME TO DO, DOES NOT COMPARE TO YOUR UNLIMITED FAVOUR. THANK YOU FOR WATCHING OVER ME HEAVENLY FATHER. I PRAY THIS IN THE PRECIOUS NAME OF JESUS AND BY THE GUIDANCE OF YOU, PRECIOUS HOLY SPIRIT. AMEN AND AMEN.

UNLIMITED

PRECIOUS LORD JESUS YOU GIVE US YOUR UNLIMITED LOVE;
PRECIOUS LORD JESUS YOU GIVE US WITH YOUR MERCIES FROM ABOVE.

PRECIOUS LORD JESUS YOU GIVE US YOUR UNLIMITED BREATH;
PRECIOUS LORD JESUS YOU GIVE US OR WE WOULD SURELY SEE DEATH.

PRECIOUS LORD JESUS YOU GIVE US YOUR UNLIMITED POWER;
PRECIOUS LORD JESUS YOU GIVE US TO SUSTAIN US EACH AND EVERY HOUR.

PRECIOUS LORD JESUS YOU GIVE US YOUR UNLIMITED GRACE;
PRECIOUS LORD JESUS YOU GIVE US SO WE CAN ENDURE THIS RACE.

PRECIOUS LORD JESUS YOU GIVE US YOUR UNLIMITED FAVOUR;
PRECIOUS LORD JESUS YOU GIVE US SO WE ARE MINDFUL OF OUR BEHAVIOUR.

PRECIOUS LORD JESUS YOU GIVE US YOUR UNLIMITED GLORY;
PRECIOUS LORD JESUS YOU GIVE US SO WE CAN TELL YOUR MERCIFUL STORY.

PRECIOUS LORD JESUS YOU GIVE US YOUR UNLIMITED LIVING WATER;
PRECIOUS LORD JESUS YOU GIVE US SO WE CAN LIVE NOW AND IN THE HEREAFTER.

HEAVENLY FATHER I THANK YOU THAT YOU ARE UNLIMITED IN EVERY ASPECT I CAN THINK OF. I THANK YOU HEAVENLY FATHER THAT EVERYTHING YOU DO IS OF UNLIMITED BENEFIT TO ME AND YOU. I THANK YOU HEAVENLY FATHER BY THE BLOOD OF JESUS CHRIST AND THE POWER OF THE HOLY SPIRIT. IN JESUS' MOST PRECIOUS NAME I PRAY. AMEN AND AMEN.

YOUR LOVE FOR ME IS COMPLETE PRECIOUS LORD JESUS

YOUR LOVE FOR ME IS COMPLETE PRECIOUS LORD JESUS, YOU GAVE ME LIFE.
YOUR LOVE FOR ME IS COMPLETE PRECIOUS LORD JESUS, YOU GAVE ME ALL THAT IS RIGHT.

YOUR LOVE FOR ME IS COMPLETE PRECIOUS LORD JESUS, YOU GAVE ME HOPE.
YOUR LOVE FOR ME IS COMPLETE PRECIOUS LORD JESUS, YOU HAVE BROADEN MY SCOPE.

YOUR LOVE FOR ME IS COMPLETE PRECIOUS LORD JESUS, YOU GAVE ME DREAMS.
YOUR LOVE FOR ME IS COMPLETE PRECIOUS LORD JESUS, YOU SHOW ME WHAT LIFE MEANS.

YOUR LOVE FOR ME IS COMPLETE PRECIOUS LORD JESUS, YOU TOOK AWAY MY SHAME.
YOUR LOVE FOR ME IS COMPLETE PRECIOUS LORD JESUS, BY THE POWER OF YOUR HOLY NAME.

YOUR LOVE FOR ME IS COMPLETE PRECIOUS LORD JESUS, YOU GAVE ME A MANSION.
YOUR LOVE FOR ME IS COMPLETE PRECIOUS LORD JESUS, TO ALL NATIONS, THIS I WILL MENTION.

YOUR LOVE FOR ME IS COMPLETE PRECIOUS LORD JESUS, HEAVEN IS MY HOME.
YOUR LOVE FOR ME IS COMPLETE PRECIOUS LORD JESUS, IN ITS' COURTS I WILL ROME.

YOUR LOVE FOR ME IS COMPLETE PRECIOUS LORD JESUS, I WILL REST IN YOUR ARMS.
YOUR LOVE FOR ME IS COMPLETE PRECIOUS LORD JESUS, I WILL ENJOY ALL OF YOUR CHARMS.

YOUR LOVE COMPLETES ME PRECIOUS LORD JESUS. "1 JOHN 3:1 SEE WHAT GREAT LOVE THE FATHER HAS LAVISHED ON US, THAT WE SHOULD BE CALLED CHILDREN OF GOD! AND THAT IS WHAT WE ARE! THE REASON THE WORLD DOES NOT KNOW US IS THAT IT DID NOT KNOW HIM." I THANK YOU FOR YOUR LOVE FOR ME HEAVENLY FATHER. I THANK YOU FOR YOUR LOVE FOR ME LORD JESUS. I THANK YOU FOR YOUR LOVE FOR ME PRECIOUS HOLY SPIRIT. I PRAY THIS IN JESUS MOST PRECIOUS NAME. AMEN AND AMEN.

I LONG TO DO THY WILL

I LONG TO DO THY WILL, HEAVENLY FATHER ABOVE;
I LONG TO DO THY WILL, HEAVENLY FATHER OF LOVE.

I LONG TO DO THY WILL, JESUS MY LORD AND SAVIOUR;
I LONG TO DO THY WILL, JESUS LORD OF MY BEHAVIOUR.

I LONG TO DO THY WILL, HEAVENLY FATHER OF MIGHT;
I LONG TO DO THY WILL, HEAVENLY FATHER WHO GIVES ME SIGHT.

I LONG TO DO THY WILL, JESUS MY LORD AND FRIEND;
I LONG TO DO THY WILL, JESUS MY LORD ON WHOM I DEPEND.

I LONG TO DO THY WILL, HEAVENLY FATHER OF LIGHT;
I LONG TO DO THY WILL, HEAVENLY FATHER WHO MAKES ALL THINGS BRIGHT.

I LONG TO DO THY WILL, JESUS MY LORD AND BROTHER;
I LONG TO DO THY WILL, JESUS MY LORD LIKE NO OTHER.

I LONG TO DO THY WILL, PRECIOUS HOLY TRINITY;
I LONG TO DO THY WILL, GOD OF ALL DIVINITY.

HEAVENLY FATHER, PRECIOUS LORD JESUS, PRECIOUS HOLY SPIRIT, I
LOVE TO DO THY WILL. PLEASE SATISFY THE HUNGER WITHIN ME TO DO THY
WILL. I PRAY THIS IN JESUS' PRECIOUS NAME. AMEN AND AMEN.

I AM SORRY PRECIOUS LORD JESUS

I AM SORRY PRECIOUS LORD JESUS FOR MY BEHAVIOUR;
I AM SORRY PRECIOUS LORD JESUS, I DID NOT REPRESENT YOU AS MY SAVIOUR.

I AM SORRY PRECIOUS LORD JESUS FOR MY FROWNING;
I AM SORRY PRECIOUS LORD JESUS, IT IS NOT REPRESENTATIVE OF A PRINCE AT HIS CROWNING.

I AM SORRY PRECIOUS LORD JESUS FOR MY ATTITUDE;
I AM SORRY PRECIOUS LORD JESUS, IT IS NOT REPRESENTATIVE OF YOUR BEATITUDES.

I AM SORRY PRECIOUS LORD JESUS FOR MY POUTING;
I AM SORRY PRECIOUS LORD JESUS, I DID NOT REPRESENT YOU WITH MY DOUBTING.

I AM SORRY PRECIOUS LORD JESUS FOR MY ANXIOUSNESS;
I AM SORRY PRECIOUS LORD JESUS, I DID NOT REPRESENT YOU AS MY RIGHTEOUSNESS.

I AM SORRY PRECIOUS LORD JESUS FOR MY LACK OF HOPE;
I AM SORRY PRECIOUS LORD JESUS, I DID NOT REPRESENT YOUR ENORMOUS SCOPE.

I AM SORRY PRECIOUS LORD JESUS FOR MY LACK OF SIGHT;
I AM SORRY PRECIOUS LORD JESUS, I DID NOT REPRESENT YOU AND ALL YOUR MIGHT.

HEAVENLY FATHER AT TIMES I GET FRUSTRATED AND I FORGET WHO YOU ARE AND WHAT THOU HAS DONE FOR ME. HOLY SPIRIT PLEASE HELP ME NEVER TO FORGET WHAT MY HEAVENLY FATHER, MY LORD AND SAVIOUR JESUS CHRIST AND YOU HAVE DONE FOR ME, IS DOING FOR ME AND WILL DO FOR ME. I PRAY THIS IN JESUS' MOST PRECIOUS NAME. AMEN AND AMEN.

YOU LOVE ME PRECIOUS LORD JESUS

YOU LOVE ME PRECIOUS LORD JESUS, WHETHER I AM A BILLIONAIRE OR WHETHER I AM JUST BREATHING FRESH AIR.

YOU LOVE ME PRECIOUS LORD JESUS, WHETHER I AM AS HIGH AS MOUNT EVEREST OR WHETHER I AM JUST LAYING DOWN TO REST.

YOU LOVE ME PRECIOUS LORD JESUS, WHETHER I AM AS GOOD AS NEW OR WHETHER I AM DEDICATED TO YOU.

YOU LOVE ME PRECIOUS LORD JESUS, WHETHER I AM DOWN AND OUT OR WHETHER I AM TELLING THE WORLD WHAT YOU ARE ALL ABOUT.

YOU LOVE ME PRECIOUS LORD JESUS, WHETHER I AM IN MY DARKEST HOUR OR WHETHER YOU ENDOW ME WITH YOUR AWESOME POWER.

YOU LOVE ME PRECIOUS LORD JESUS, WHETHER I AM A BIG DISGRACE OR WHETHER I AM FILLED WITH YOUR AMAZING GRACE.

YOU LOVE ME PRECIOUS LORD JESUS, WHETHER I AM BEGGING YOU PLEASE OR WHETHER I AM RISING FROM MY KNEES.

I THANK YOU HEAVENLY FATHER, I THANK YOU PRECIOUS LORD JESUS, I THANK YOU PRECIOUS HOLY SPIRIT FOR LOVING ME JUST AS I AM. I WANT TO LET THE WORLD KNOW HEAVENLY FATHER THAT YOUR LOVE IS UNCONDITIONAL. I CAN ONLY DO THIS BY THE PRECIOUS BLOOD OF JESUS AND THE EMPOWERING OF YOU, PRECIOUS HOLY SPIRIT. I ASK AND PRAY IN JESUS' MOST PRECIOUS NAME. AMEN AND AMEN.

HELP ME TO REMEMBER HOW GOOD YOU ARE TO ME PRECIOUS LORD JESUS

WHEN THINGS DO NOT GO MY WAY, HELP ME TO REMEMBER HOW GOOD YOU ARE TO ME PRECIOUS LORD JESUS.

WHEN I AM SAD AND HAVE GONE ASTRAY, HELP ME TO REMEMBER HOW GOOD YOU ARE TO ME PRECIOUS LORD JESUS.

WHEN I AM HAPPY AND CARE FREE, HELP ME TO REMEMBER HOW GOOD YOU ARE TO ME PRECIOUS LORD JESUS.

WHEN I RISE WITH THE RADIANT SUN, HELP ME TO REMEMBER HOW GOOD YOU ARE TO ME PRECIOUS LORD JESUS.

WHEN I AM UP AND WHEN I AM DOWN, HELP ME TO REMEMBER HOW GOOD YOU ARE TO ME PRECIOUS LORD JESUS.

WHEN I LAY IN MY BED AT NIGHT, HELP ME TO REMEMBER HOW GOOD YOU ARE TO ME PRECIOUS LORD JESUS.

WHEN MY TIME ON EARTH IS DONE, I WILL REMEMBER HOW GOOD YOU HAVE BEEN TO ME PRECIOUS LORD JESUS.

I THANK YOU FOR BEING SO GOOD TO ME PRECIOUS LORD JESUS. THERE IS NO GOD LIKE YOU HEAVENLY FATHER. THERE IS NO COMFORTER LIKE YOU HOLY SPIRIT. TEACH ME TO REMEMBER AT ALL TIMES PRECIOUS HOLY SPIRIT HOW GOOD MY HEAVENLY FATHER IS, HOW GOOD MY LORD AND SAVIOUR JESUS IS. I ASK AND PRAY THIS IN JESUS' MOST PRECIOUS NAME. AMEN AND AMEN.

PRECIOUS LORD JESUS I AM TRYING TO MAKE SENSE OF IT ALL

PRECIOUS LORD JESUS I AM TRYING TO MAKE SENSE OF IT ALL, WHY DO WE CHOOSE DEATH INSTEAD OF YOUR LIFE GIVING BREATH?

PRECIOUS LORD JESUS I AM TRYING TO MAKE SENSE OF IT ALL, WHY DO WE HATE INSTEAD OF APPRECIATING ALL THAT YOU MAKE GREAT?

PRECIOUS LORD JESUS I AM TRYING TO MAKE SENSE OF IT ALL, WHY DO WE BLAME YOU FOR ALL THE DISASTER THAT WE DO?

PRECIOUS LORD JESUS I AM TRYING TO MAKE SENSE OF IT ALL, WHY DO WE FIGHT INSTEAD OF MAKING THINGS RIGHT?

PRECIOUS LORD JESUS I AM TRYING TO MAKE SENSE OF IT ALL, WHY DO WE FALL INSTEAD OF ANSWERING YOUR CALL?

PRECIOUS LORD JESUS I AM TRYING TO MAKE SENSE OF IT ALL, WHY DO WE KILL INSTEAD OF DOING THY PERFECT WILL?

PRECIOUS LORD JESUS I AM TRYING TO MAKE SENSE OF IT ALL, WHY DO WE LIVE, IS IT BY THE BREATH THAT YOU GIVE?

HEAVENLY FATHER HELP ME TO MAKE SENSE OF IT ALL. I NEED YOUR GUIDANCE PRECIOUS HOLY SPIRIT TO ACCOMPLISH THE WILL OF MY HEAVENLY FATHER. I AM ASKING THIS IN THE MOST PRECIOUS NAME OF JESUS. AMEN AND AMEN.

I TURN MY EYES TO YOU PRECIOUS LORD JESUS

I TURN MY EYES TO YOU PRECIOUS LORD JESUS, LET YOUR HOLY FACE BE MY DWELLING PLACE.

I TURN MY EYES TO YOU PRECIOUS LORD JESUS, LET YOUR WARM EMBRACE BE MY AMAZING GRACE.

I TURN MY EYES TO YOU PRECIOUS LORD JESUS, LET YOUR HOLY HEART BE MINE FROM THE VERY START.

I TURN MY EYES TO YOU PRECIOUS LORD JESUS, LET YOUR UNFAILING LOVE REST ON ME LIKE A GENTLE DOVE.

I TURN MY EYES TO YOU PRECIOUS LORD JESUS, LET YOUR AWESOME POWER EMBRACE ME EACH AND EVERY HOUR.

I TURN MY EYES TO YOU PRECIOUS LORD JESUS, LET YOUR CREATION DECLARE YOUR GLORY SO NEAR.

I TURN MY EYES TO YOU PRECIOUS LORD JESUS, LET YOUR KINGDOM COME AND LET THY WILL BE DONE.

PRECIOUS LORD JESUS I TURN MY EYES TO YOU, WHAT ELSE CAN I DO? I GIVE YOU PRAISE HEAVENLY FATHER AND I THANK YOU PRECIOUS HOLY SPIRIT. I PRAY THIS IN JESUS' MOST PRECIOUS NAME. AMEN AND AMEN.

LIKE YOU PRECIOUS JESUS

I WANT TO LIVE LIKE YOU LIVE, PRECIOUS LORD JESUS.

I WANT TO LOVE LIKE YOU LOVE, PRECIOUS LORD JESUS.

I WANT TO SMILE LIKE YOU SMILE, PRECIOUS LORD JESUS.

I WANT TO HOPE LIKE YOU HOPE, PRECIOUS LORD JESUS.

I WANT TO PRAY LIKE YOU PRAY, PRECIOUS LORD JESUS.

I WANT TO BLESS LIKE YOU BLESS, PRECIOUS LORD JESUS.

I WANT TO CARE LIKE YOU CARE, PRECIOUS LORD JESUS.

I WANT TO ACT LIKE YOU ACT, PRECIOUS LORD JESUS.

I WANT TO SEEK LIKE YOU SEEK, PRECIOUS LORD JESUS.

I WANT TO BELIEVE LIKE YOU BELIEVE, PRECIOUS LORD JESUS.

I WANT TO GIVE LIKE YOU GIVE, PRECIOUS LORD JESUS.

I WANT TO BE LIKE YOU, PRECIOUS LORD JESUS.

PRECIOUS HOLY SPIRIT, PLEASE TEACH ME HOW TO BECOME MORE LIKE JESUS. THIS I ASK IN JESUS' MOST PRECIOUS NAME. AMEN AND AMEN.

WHAT WE TALK ABOUT

WE TALK MORE ABOUT DISASTER RATHER THAN YOU BEING OUR MASTER, PRECIOUS LORD JESUS.

WE TALK MORE ABOUT HATE RATHER THAN THE PRECIOUS LIFE THAT YOU MAKE, PRECIOUS LORD JESUS.

WE TALK MORE ABOUT DOOM RATHER THAN THE ROOM YOU HAVE PREPARED FOR US, PRECIOUS LORD JESUS.

WE TALK MORE ABOUT DEFEAT RATHER THAN THE SWEET RETREAT WE HAVE IN YOU, PRECIOUS LORD JESUS.

WE TALK MORE ABOUT STRIFE RATHER THAN THE QUALITY OF LIFE WE HAVE IN YOU, PRECIOUS LORD JESUS.

WE TALK MORE ABOUT THE DROUGHT RATHER THAN WHAT YOU ARE ALL ABOUT, PRECIOUS LORD JESUS.

WE TALK MORE ABOUT DEATH RATHER THAN OUR DAILY BREATH THAT YOU GIVE TO US, PRECIOUS LORD JESUS.

PLEASE TEACH ME PRECIOUS LORD JESUS TO TALK MORE ABOUT YOU RATHER THAN THE THINGS WE CANNOT DO. YOU, PRECIOUS LORD JESUS, ARE THE WAY, THE TRUTH AND THE LIFE. TEACH ME TO HONOUR YOU IN ALL THAT I DO. I PRAY THIS IN YOUR MOST PRECIOUS NAME LORD JESUS. AMEN AND AMEN.

PRECIOUS LORD JESUS, BE MY FIRST LOVE

AS I STRUGGLE TO GET UP FROM MY BED AND I REALIZE THAT I AM NOT DEAD, I AM ASKING YOU PRECIOUS LORD JESUS TO BE MY FIRST LOVE.

AS I STRUGGLE TO SAY MY PRAYER AND MY WORDS ARE OH SO DIRE, I AM ASKING YOU PRECIOUS LORD JESUS TO BE MY FIRST LOVE.

AS I STRUGGLE TO READ YOUR HOLY BOOK AND I REALIZE HOW HORRIBLE I LOOK, I AM ASKING YOU PRECIOUS LORD JESUS TO BE MY FIRST LOVE.

AS I STRUGGLE THROUGH THE FIRST PART OF MY DAY AND I CAN NOT FIND THE RIGHT WORDS TO SAY, I AM ASKING YOU PRECIOUS LORD JESUS TO BE MY FIRST LOVE.

AS I STRUGGLE TO APPROACH THE NOON HOUR AND FIND I AM RUNNING OUT OF POWER, I AM ASKING YOU PRECIOUS LORD JESUS TO BE MY FIRST LOVE.

AS I STRUGGLE TO ACCOMPLISH ALL MY TASKS AND I CAN NOT REMEMBER WHAT WAS ASKED, I AM ASKING YOU PRECIOUS LORD JESUS TO BE MY FIRST LOVE.

AS I STRUGGLE TO BRING THE DAY TO A CLOSE AND I FEEL SO TWISTED LIKE A RUBBER HOSE, I AM ASKING YOU PRECIOUS LORD JESUS TO BE MY FIRST LOVE.

YOUR LOVE PRECIOUS LORD JESUS IS AMAZING. PRECIOUS HOLY SPIRIT PLEASE TEACH ME HOW TO MAKE MY HEAVENLY FATHER, MY PRECIOUS LORD JESUS AND YOU HOLY COMFORTER, MY FIRST LOVE. I ASK THIS IN THE MIGHTY NAME OF JESUS. AMEN AND AMEN.

LET GO

LET GO OF ANGER. JESUS WILL HELP YOU AVOID ALL THE ANGUISH AND SLANDER.

LET GO OF HATE. JESUS WILL HELP YOU, ON HIM YOU SHOULD MEDITATE.

LET GO OF STRIFE. JESUS WILL HELP YOU, GIVE HIM THE BEST OF YOUR LIFE.

LET GO OF ILL WILL. JESUS WILL HELP YOU TO ABIDE WITH HIM STILL.

LET GO OF DOUBT. JESUS WILL HELP YOU, HE WILL TELL YOU WHAT LIFE IS ALL ABOUT.

LET GO OF FEAR. JESUS WILL HELP YOU, TRY HIM IF YOU DARE.

LET GO OF THE PAST. JESUS WILL HELP YOU, HE IS THE FIRST AND THE LAST.

PRECIOUS LORD JESUS, PLEASE TEACH ME HOW TO LET GO AND FALL INTO YOUR ARMS. IN YOUR ARMS I AM PROTECTED FROM ALL EVILS AND HARMS. I TRUST YOU PRECIOUS LORD JESUS. PLEASE LEAD ME TO WHAT I MUST DO. IN YOUR PRECIOUS NAME I ASK THIS JESUS. AMEN AND AMEN.

I AM TIRED PRECIOUS LORD JESUS

I AM TIRED PRECIOUS LORD JESUS, BUT I AM WILLING TO FIGHT.
I AM TIRED PRECIOUS LORD JESUS, PLEASE BLESS ME WITH YOUR MIGHT.

I AM TIRED PRECIOUS LORD JESUS, BUT I AM WILLING TO STAND.
I AM TIRED PRECIOUS LORD JESUS, PLEASE BLESS ME WITH YOUR HELPING HAND.

I AM TIRED PRECIOUS LORD JESUS, BUT I AM WILLING TO GO.
I AM TIRED PRECIOUS LORD JESUS, PLEASE BLESS ME SO I CAN GROW.

I AM TIRED PRECIOUS LORD JESUS, BUT I AM WILLING TO GIVE.
I AM TIRED PRECIOUS LORD JESUS, PLEASE BLESS ME SO I CAN LIVE.

I AM TIRED PRECIOUS LORD JESUS, BUT I AM WILLING TO SPEAK.
I AM TIRED PRECIOUS LORD JESUS, PLEASE BLESS ME WHEN I AM WEAK.

I AM TIRED PRECIOUS LORD JESUS, BUT I AM WILLING TO PRAY.
I AM TIRED PRECIOUS LORD JESUS, PLEASE BLESS ME EACH AND EVERY DAY.

I AM TIRED PRECIOUS LORD JESUS, BUT I AM WILLING TO SHARE.
I AM TIRED PRECIOUS LORD JESUS, PLEASE BLESS ME AND I WILL TELL THE WORLD HOW MUCH YOU CARE.

PRECIOUS LORD JESUS, I AM TIRED BUT BECAUSE YOU CARE, PLEASE DRAW ME NEAR TO YOU SO I CAN TELL THE WORLD ALL ABOUT WHAT YOU CAN DO. PRECIOUS LORD JESUS MY ONLY COMFORT IS IN YOU. I THANK YOU FROM THE BOTTOM OF MY HEART FOR BEING SO TRUE TO ME PRECIOUS LORD JESUS. AMEN AND AMEN.

IT MATTERS TO YOU PRECIOUS LORD JESUS

IF I HAVE NO DAILY BREAD.
IF I HAVE NO PLACE TO LAY MY HEAD.
IT MATTERS TO YOU PRECIOUS LORD JESUS.

IF I HAVE NO MORE TO GIVE.
IF I HAVE NO REASON TO LIVE.
IT MATTERS TO YOU PRECIOUS LORD JESUS.

IF I AM TIRED AND WORN.
IF I AM WEARING MY OLD FROWN.
IT MATTERS TO YOU PRECIOUS LORD JESUS.

IF I AM TROUBLED THROUGHOUT THE DAY.
IF I HAVE NO MORE WORDS TO SAY.
IT MATTERS TO YOU PRECIOUS LORD JESUS.

IF I AM LOOKING UP TO YOU.
IF I AM ASKING WHAT CAN I DO.
IT MATTERS TO YOU PRECIOUS LORD JESUS.

IF I HAVE GIVEN IT MY ALL.
IF I CAN NOT ANSWER WHEN YOU CALL.
IT MATTERS TO YOU PRECIOUS LORD JESUS.

IF I HAVE TURNED FROM YOUR ETERNAL WILL.
IF I HAVE REFUSED TO SIT AND BE STILL.
IT MATTERS TO YOU PRECIOUS LORD JESUS.

PRECIOUS LORD JESUS, EVERYTHING MATTERS TO YOU. YOU KNOW OUR
RISING UP AND YOU KNOW OUR SITTING DOWN. YOU KNOW WHEN WE ARE
SAD, YOU KNOW WHEN WE ARE MAD. YOU KNOW THE HAIRS ON OUR HEAD
AND YOU KNOW WHAT WORDS WE HAVE JUST SAID. PLEASE TEACH US TO
BE MINDFUL OF YOU, PRECIOUS LORD JESUS. AMEN AND AMEN.

IN HIS PRESENCE

IN HIS PRESENCE THERE IS JOY DIVINE.
IN HIS PRESENCE THAT JOY IS YOURS AND MINE.

IN HIS PRESENCE THERE IS HOPE.
IN HIS PRESENCE THERE IS PLENTY OF HOPE SO YOU AND I CAN COPE.

IN HIS PRESENCE THERE IS LOVE.
IN HIS PRESENCE THERE IS PLENTY OF LOVE SENT FROM OUR FATHER UP ABOVE.

IN HIS PRESENCE THERE IS GRACE.
IN HIS PRESENCE THERE IS PLENTY OF GRACE SHINING FROM HIS AMAZING FACE.

IN HIS PRESENCE THERE IS LIFE.
IN HIS PRESENCE THERE IS PLENTY OF LIFE FOR YOUR LOVELY WIFE.

IN HIS PRESENCE THERE IS A TOMORROW.
IN HIS PRESENCE THERE IS PLENTY FOR TOMORROW WITHOUT ANY SORROW.

IN HIS PRESENCE THERE IS PEACE.
IN HIS PRESENCE THERE IS PLENTY OF PEACE UNDERNEATH HIS EVERLASTING FLEECE.

I NEED TO BE IN YOUR PRESENCE PRECIOUS LORD JESUS MY LORD AND MASTER. PLEASE SHOWER ME WITH YOUR PRESENCE PRECIOUS LORD JESUS, SO I CAN ALSO SHOW OTHERS. I ASK THIS IN YOUR PRECIOUS NAME JESUS. AMEN AND AMEN.

PLEASE OPEN ME PRECIOUS LORD JESUS

PLEASE OPEN MY EYES THAT I MAY SEE WHAT PRECIOUS GIFTS YOU HAVE IN STORE FOR ME PRECIOUS LORD JESUS.

PLEASE OPEN MY EARS THAT I MAY HEAR WHAT PRECIOUS WORDS YOU WHISPER WHEN YOU ARE NEAR PRECIOUS LORD JESUS.

PLEASE OPEN MY MOUTH THAT I MAY SHOUT OUT WHAT YOU ARE ALL ABOUT PRECIOUS LORD JESUS.

PLEASE OPEN MY HAND THAT I MAY GIVE AND LET OTHERS LIVE BY YOUR PLAN PRECIOUS LORD JESUS.

PLEASE OPEN MY HEART THAT I MAY HAVE A BRAND NEW START PRECIOUS LORD JESUS.

PLEASE OPEN MY MIND THAT I MAY SHOW YOU ARE ONE OF A KIND PRECIOUS LORD JESUS.

PLEASE OPEN ME THAT I MAY BE A REFLECTION OF THEE PRECIOUS LORD JESUS.

PLEASE OPEN ME TO THE WONDERFUL THINGS YOU HAVE IN YOUR ABUNDANT STOREHOUSE PRECIOUS HOLY FATHER. PLEASE TEACH ME HOW TO PARTAKE OF YOUR STOREHOUSE PRECIOUS LORD JESUS. PLEASE TEACH ME HOW TO IMPART TO OTHERS OF YOUR STOREHOUSE PRECIOUS HOLY SPIRIT. I ASK THIS IN JESUS MOST PRECIOUS NAME. AMEN AND AMEN.

I AM ON MY KNEES PRECIOUS JESUS

I AM ON MY KNEES PRECIOUS JESUS. PLEASE WHISPER IN MY EAR AND TELL ME HOW MUCH YOU CARE.

I AM ON MY KNEES PRECIOUS JESUS. PLEASE HELP ME WHEN I FALL AND PLEASE ANSWER WHEN I CALL.

I AM ON MY KNEES PRECIOUS JESUS. PLEASE SEND A MESSAGE FROM ABOVE BECAUSE I AM DESPERATE FOR YOUR UNFAILING LOVE.

I AM ON MY KNEES PRECIOUS JESUS. PLEASE MAKE ME BOLD AND LET YOUR WONDERFUL STORY BE TOLD.

I AM ON MY KNEES PRECIOUS JESUS. PLEASE GIVE ME YOUR GRACE AS I LOOK INTO YOUR AMAZING FACE.

I AM ON MY KNEES PRECIOUS JESUS. PLEASE PLEASE RESCUE ME SO YOU CAN SET ME FREE.

I AM ON MY KNEES PRECIOUS JESUS. PLEASE BLESS ME NOW AS I KNEEL DOWN AND TAKE A BOW.

I AM THANKFUL THAT YOU HEAR ME AS I AM ON MY KNEES PRECIOUS JESUS. I KNOW YOU CARE AND I KNOW YOU ARE EVER SO NEAR. I THANK YOU PRECIOUS JESUS NOW AND ALWAYS. AMEN AND AMEN.

IN YOUR PRESENCE PRECIOUS JESUS

IN YOUR PRESENCE PRECIOUS JESUS, I FEEL YOUR RADIANT PEACE.

IN YOUR PRESENCE PRECIOUS JESUS, I FEEL YOUR RADIANT LOVE.

IN YOUR PRESENCE PRECIOUS JESUS, I FEEL YOUR RADIANT HOPE.

IN YOUR PRESENCE PRECIOUS JESUS, I FEEL YOUR RADIANT MERCY.

IN YOUR PRESENCE PRECIOUS JESUS, I FEEL YOUR RADIANT GRACE.

IN YOUR PRESENCE PRECIOUS JESUS, I FEEL YOUR RADIANT TRUTH.

IN YOUR PRESENCE PRECIOUS JESUS, I FEEL YOUR RADIANCE.

PRECIOUS JESUS AS I REACH OUT TO YOU IN THE EARLY MORNING, I FEEL YOUR RADIANCE EVER SO NEAR. MY HOPE IS THAT YOUR PRESENCE WILL NEVER DEPART. THIS IS MY PRAYER AND MY DESIRE IN JESUS NAME. AMEN AND AMEN.

I NEED YOUR PRESENCE

I NEED YOUR PRESENCE TO SURROUND ME, SO I COULD LIVE SECURELY WITH THEE.

I NEED YOUR PRESENCE TO MOULD ME, SO I COULD BE MORE AND MORE LIKE THEE.

I NEED YOUR PRESENCE TO HOLD ME, SO I COULD BE OH SO BOLD FOR THEE.

I NEED YOUR PRESENCE TO LEAD ME, SO I COULD FOLLOW ONLY AFTER THEE.

I NEED YOUR PRESENCE TO LOVE ME, SO I COULD PLACE NO ONE ABOVE THEE.

I NEED YOUR PRESENCE TO BLESS ME, SO I COULD GIVE MY BEST TO THEE.

I NEED YOUR PRESENCE TO MOVE ME, SO I COULD BE USED ONLY FOR THEE.

IN YOUR PRESENCE PRECIOUS LORD JESUS, I FEEL COMPLETE. YOUR LOVE COVERS ALL MY IMPERFECTIONS PRECIOUS LORD JESUS. MY DESIRE IS TO REMAIN IN YOUR PRESENCE PRECIOUS LORD JESUS. AMEN AND AMEN.

PLEASE FORGIVE ME PRECIOUS JESUS

PLEASE FORGIVE ME FOR NOT STICKING TO YOUR PLAN PRECIOUS JESUS. I TRULY DID NOT UNDERSTAND IT PRECIOUS JESUS.

PLEASE FORGIVE ME FOR NOT TRUSTING IN YOUR WAY PRECIOUS JESUS. I WAS GIVEN INTO MY SILLY SWAY PRECIOUS JESUS.

PLEASE FORGIVE ME OF MY UNBELIEF PRECIOUS JESUS. PLEASE HELP ME TO TURN OVER A BRAND NEW LEAF PRECIOUS JESUS.

PLEASE FORGIVE ME FOR MY DOUBTING YOU PRECIOUS JESUS. I SHOULD HAVE BEEN SHOUTING OUT ALL ABOUT YOU PRECIOUS JESUS.

PLEASE FORGIVE ME FOR MY LACK OF HOPE PRECIOUS JESUS. I UNDERESTIMATE YOUR ENORMOUS SCOPE PRECIOUS JESUS.

PLEASE FORGIVE ME FOR MY SHORT SIGHT PRECIOUS JESUS. I WAS UNAWARE OF YOUR AWESOME MIGHT PRECIOUS JESUS.

PLEASE FORGIVE ME FOR WHAT I DO PRECIOUS JESUS. MY ONLY HOPE REMAINS IN YOU PRECIOUS JESUS.

I THANK YOU PRECIOUS JESUS FOR ALL THAT YOU DO. MY LIFE WOULD HAVE NO MEANING WITHOUT YOU. YOU PRECIOUS JESUS HAVE LIFTED ME UP TO ACCOMPLISH GREAT AND MIGHTY THINGS FOR YOUR EVERLASTING KINGDOM. I THANK YOU FOR MAKING ME A PART OF YOUR PLAN PRECIOUS JESUS. I ACCEPT THIS IN YOUR MIGHTY NAME PRECIOUS JESUS. AMEN AND AMEN.

PRECIOUS JESUS YOU ARE MY TREASURE

PRECIOUS JESUS YOU ARE MY UNENDING TREASURE AND IN YOU I WILL HAVE ALL MY PLEASURE.

PRECIOUS JESUS YOU ARE MY UNENDING HOPE AND IN YOU I WILL BROADEN MY SCOPE.

PRECIOUS JESUS YOU ARE MY UNENDING WAY AND IN YOU I WILL HAVE MY SWAY.

PRECIOUS JESUS YOU ARE MY UNENDING FRIEND AND IN YOU I WILL HAVE NO END.

PRECIOUS JESUS YOU ARE MY UNENDING LIGHT AND IN YOU I WILL DO ALL THAT IS RIGHT.

PRECIOUS JESUS YOU ARE MY UNENDING MIGHT AND IN YOU I WILL HAVE SET MY SIGHT.

PRECIOUS JESUS YOU ARE MY UNENDING LOVE AND IN YOU I WILL NESTLE LIKE A DOVE.

PRECIOUS JESUS YOU ARE ENDLESS. PLEASE HELP ME TO DEPEND ON YOU MORE AND MORE EACH DAY. PLEASE HELP ME NEVER TO SWAY. HELP ME PRECIOUS JESUS TO PARTAKE OF YOUR UNENDING TREASURES AT YOUR RIGHT HAND. IN YOUR NAME I PRAY THIS, PRECIOUS JESUS. AMEN AND AMEN.

ALL IN YOU PRECIOUS JESUS

IN YOU THERE IS ALL LOVE PRECIOUS JESUS.

IN YOU THERE IS ALL HOPE PRECIOUS JESUS.

IN YOU THERE IS ALL PEACE PRECIOUS JESUS.

IN YOU THERE IS ALL MIGHT PRECIOUS JESUS.

IN YOU THERE IS ALL STRENGTH PRECIOUS JESUS.

IN YOU THERE IS ALL WISDOM PRECIOUS JESUS.

IN YOU THERE IS ALL KNOWLEDGE AND UNDERSTANDING PRECIOUS JESUS.

YOU LACK NOTHING PRECIOUS JESUS. WHATEVER I NEED I HAVE IT IN YOU PRECIOUS JESUS. I AM CONVINCED OF THAT BY THE REVELATION OF YOU PRECIOUS HOLY SPIRIT. I KNOW THIS BECAUSE OF YOUR PRECIOUS NAME LORD JESUS. AMEN AND AMEN.

THANK YOU FOR PROVIDING
FOR ME PRECIOUS JESUS

THANK YOU FOR PROVIDING MY SPIRITUAL NEEDS PRECIOUS JESUS, WITHOUT WHICH I WOULD BE FULL OF MISDEEDS PRECIOUS JESUS.

THANK YOU FOR SUPPLYING MY DAILY BREAD PRECIOUS JESUS, WITHOUT WHICH I WOULD SURELY BE DEAD PRECIOUS JESUS.

THANK YOU FOR PROVIDING MY DAILY SHELTER PRECIOUS JESUS, WITHOUT WHICH I WOULD BE LIKE METAL IN A SMELTER PRECIOUS JESUS.

THANK YOU FOR BEING MY DAILY GUIDE PRECIOUS JESUS, WITHOUT WHICH I WOULD SURLEY HAVE TO RUN AND HIDE PRECIOUS JESUS.

THANK YOU FOR BEING MY DAILY HOPE PRECIOUS JESUS, WITHOUT WHICH I COULD NOT COPE PRECIOUS JESUS.

THANK YOU FOR GIVING ME MY DAILY HEALTH PRECIOUS JESUS, WITHOUT WHICH I WOULD HAVE NO HEALTH PRECIOUS JESUS.

THANK YOU FOR GIVING ME YOUR DAILY LOVE PRECIOUS JESUS, WITHOUT WHICH I WOULD FLUTTER LIKE A WOUNDED DOVE PRECIOUS JESUS.

I THANK YOU PRECIOUS LORD JESUS FOR YOUR DAILY PROVIDENCE, WITHOUT WHICH I COULD NOT EXIST. PRECIOUS HOLY SPIRIT PLEASE TEACH ME HOW TO DELIGHT MYSELF IN MY PRECIOUS HEAVENLY FATHER, IN MY PRECIOUS LORD JESUS AND IN YOU PRECIOUS HOLY SPIRIT AND PLEASE GRANT ME THE DESIRES OF MY HEART. AMEN AND AMEN.

I DON'T WANT WHAT THE WORLD HAVE PRECIOUS JESUS

I DON'T WANT WHAT THE WORLD HAVE PRECIOUS JESUS, I WANT WHAT YOU HAVE PRECIOUS JESUS.

I DON'T WANT WHAT THE WORLD GIVES PRECIOUS JESUS, I WANT WHAT YOU GIVE PRECIOUS JESUS.

I DON'T WANT WHAT THE WORLD CRAVES PRECIOUS JESUS, I WANT WHAT YOU CRAVE PRECIOUS JESUS.

I DON'T WANT WHAT THE WORLD POSSESS PRECIOUS JESUS, I WANT WHAT YOU POSSESS PRECIOUS JESUS.

I DON'T WANT WHAT THE WORLD SEEKS PRECIOUS JESUS, I WANT WHAT YOU SEEK PRECIOUS JESUS.

I DON'T WANT WHAT THE WORLD WORSHIPS PRECIOUS JESUS, I WANT TO WORSHIP YOU PRECIOUS JESUS.

I DON'T WANT WHAT THE WORLD LOVES PRECIOUS JESUS, I WANT WHAT YOU LOVE PRECIOUS JESUS.

PRECIOUS JESUS, I DON'T WANT WHAT THE WORLD HAVE, I WANT WHAT YOU HAVE. WHAT YOU HAVE PRECIOUS JESUS IS ETERNAL AND THAT IS WHAT I WANT MORE THAN ANYTHING PRECIOUS JESUS. AMEN AND AMEN.

WORK YOUR MIRACLES IN ME PRECIOUS JESUS

PLEASE WORK YOUR MIRACLE OF LIFE IN ME PRECIOUS JESUS. PLEASE CUT ME AND MOULD ME WITH YOUR SURGEONS KNIFE PRECIOUS JESUS.

PLEASE WORK YOUR MIRACLE OF GRACE IN ME PRECIOUS JESUS. PLEASE DRAW ME NEAR TO YOUR WELCOMING FACE PRECIOUS JESUS.

PLEASE WORK YOUR MIRACLE OF MERCY IN ME PRECIOUS JESUS. PLEASE FILL ME WITH YOUR UNENDING BURSARY PRECIOUS JESUS.

PLEASE WORK YOUR MIRACLE OF HEALTH IN ME PRECIOUS JESUS. PLEASE SHOWER ME WITH YOUR ENORMOUS WEALTH PRECIOUS JESUS.

PLEASE WORK YOUR MIRACLE OF INSIGHT IN ME PRECIOUS JESUS. PLEASE MAKE ALL MY DAYS ON EARTH ALWAYS BRIGHT PRECIOUS JESUS.

PLEASE WORK YOUR MIRACLE OF BEAUTY IN ME PRECIOUS JESUS. PLEASE HELP ME TO FULFILL MY GODLY DUTY PRECIOUS JESUS.

PLEASE WORK YOUR MIRACLE OF LOVE IN ME PRECIOUS JESUS. PLEASE LET IT RAIN DOWN FROM HEAVEN ABOVE PRECIOUS JESUS.

I THANK YOU PRECIOUS JESUS FOR YOUR MIRACLES IN MY LIFE. EVERY ASPECT OF MY LIFE REFLECTS YOUR UNENDING LOVE AND MERCIES TOWARDS ME. PRECIOUS JESUS I AM GRATEFUL TOWARDS YOU AND FOR ALL THAT YOU DO. I GIVE YOU THANKS AND PRAISE PRECIOUS JESUS. AMEN AND MEN.

IN YOU THERE IS NO ROOM TO FAIL PRECIOUS JESUS

IN YOU THERE IS NO ROOM TO FAIL PRECIOUS JESUS; BECAUSE YOU HAVE DIRECTED ME TO YOUR EVERLASTING TRAIL PRECIOUS JESUS.

IN YOU THERE IS NO ROOM TO FALL PRECIOUS JESUS; BECAUSE YOU HAVE ANSWERED EACH AND EVERYONE OF MY CALL PRECIOUS JESUS.

IN YOU THERE IS NO ROOM TO POUT PRECIOUS JESUS; BECAUSE YOU HAVE TAKEN AWAY ALL OF MY DOUBT PRECIOUS JESUS.

IN YOU THERE IS NO ROOM TO COWER PRECIOUS JESUS; BECAUSE YOU HAVE PLACED WITHIN ME YOUR ETERNAL POWER PRECIOUS JESUS.

IN YOU THERE IS NO ROOM TO BE AFRAID PRECIOUS JESUS; BECAUSE IN YOU I AM PERFECTLY MADE PRECIOUS JESUS.

IN YOU THERE IS NO ROOM TO SCURRY PRECIOUS JESUS; BECAUSE YOU HAVE TAKEN AWAY MY WORRY PRECIOUS JESUS.

IN YOU THERE IS NO ROOM TO NEED PRECIOUS JESUS; BECAUSE YOU HAVE PLACED WITHIN ME YOUR ETERNAL SEED PRECIOUS JESUS.

I THANK YOU PRECIOUS JESUS THAT WITH YOU THERE IS NO ROOM TO FAIL. ALL THAT MY HEART DESIRES IS WITHIN YOU PRECIOUS JESUS. YOU ARE ALL THAT I NEED PRECIOUS JESUS. I THANK YOU AND PRAISE YOU PRECIOUS JESUS, NOW AND ALWAYS. AMEN AND ANEN.

I AM ALL YOURS PRECIOUS JESUS

THESE HANDS ARE ALL YOURS PRECIOUS JESUS. PLEASE HELP ME TO UNDERSTAND YOUR PLAN PRECIOUS JESUS.

THESE EYES ARE ALL YOURS PRECIOUS JESUS. PLEASE HELP ME TO FOCUS ON YOUR ETERNAL PRIZE PRECIOUS JESUS.

THESE FEET ARE YOURS PRECIOUS JESUS. PLEASE LEAD ME TO YOUR SWEET RETREAT PRECIOUS JESUS.

THIS MOUTH IS ALL YOURS PRECIOUS JESUS. PLEASE HELP ME TO SPREAD THE GOOD NEWS TO THE NORTH, TO THE EAST, TO THE WEST AND TO THE SOUTH PRECIOUS JESUS.

THIS HEART IS YOURS PRECIOUS JESUS. PLEASE HELP ME TO GIVE YOU MY BEST RIGHT FROM THE VERY START PRECIOUS JESUS.

THIS MIND IS YOURS PRECIOUS JESUS. PLEASE HELP ME NEVER TO BE UNKIND PRECIOUS JESUS.

THIS LOVE IS YOURS PRECIOUS JESUS. PLEASE CARESS ME LIKE A GENTLE DOVE PRECIOUS JESUS.

PRECIOUS JESUS MY LIFE IS UNFULFILLED WITHOUT YOU. PRECIOUS JESUS PLEASE TAKE PRECEDENCE IN EVERY AREA OF MY LIFE AND DELIVER ME FROM THE EVERYDAY STIFE. I GIVE YOU PRAISE AND GLORY AND ALL HONOUR PRECIOUS JESUS. AMEN AND AMEN.

PRECIOUS JESUS WHEN I HAVE

PRECIOUS JESUS WHEN I HAVE TROUBLE. YOU TAKE AWAY ALL MY TROUBLES AND BURY THEM WITH YOUR ETERNAL SHOVEL.

PRECIOUS JESUS WHEN I HAVE PAIN. YOU TAKE AWAY ALL MY PAIN AND BLESS ME TIME AND TIME AGAIN.

PRECIOUS JESUS WHEN I HAVE DOUBT. YOU TAKE AWAY ALL MY DOUBTS AND SHOW ME WHAT YOUR LIFE IS ALL ABOUT.

PRECIOUS JESUS WHEN I HAVE FEAR. YOU TAKE AWAY ALL MY FEARS AND SHOW ME HOW MUCH YOU CARE.

PRECIOUS JESUS WHEN I HAVE SORROW. YOU TAKE AWAY ALL MY SORROWS AND GIVE ME A BRIGHTER TOMORROW.

PRECIOUS JESUS WHEN I HAVE SHAME. YOU TAKE AWAY ALL MY SHAME BY THE POWER OF YOUR MIGHTY NAME.

PRECIOUS JESUS WHEN I HAVE NEED. YOU TAKE AWAY ALL MY NEEDS AND REPLENISH ME WITH YOUR EVERLASTING SEED.

PRECIOUS JESUS WHEN I HAVE YOU, THERE IS NOTHING IN THIS WORLD THAT I CANNOT DO. WHEN I SAY YOUR NAME, I AM STRENGTHEN TIME AND TIME AGAIN. I LOOK EXPECTANTLY TO YOU TO SATISFY ALL MY NEEDS ACCORDING TO YOUR ETERNAL RICHES AND GLORY. IN YOUR NAME PRECIOUS JESUS I PRAY. AMEN AND AMEN.

PRECIOUS JESUS PLEASE TAKE CARE

PRECIOUS JESUS PLEASE TAKE CARE. I AM DESPERATE FOR YOUR LOVE, PLEASE DRAW NEAR.

PRECIOUS JESUS PLEASE TAKE CARE. I AM DESPERATE FOR YOUR COMFORT, PLEASE SHOW ME HOW MUCH YOU CARE.

PRECIOUS JESUS PLEASE TAKE CARE. I AM DESPERATE FOR YOUR BLESSINGS, PLEASE SHOW ME YOUR LIFE'S LESSONS.

PRECIOUS JESUS PLEASE TAKE CARE. I AM DESPERATE FOR YOUR TENDER TOUCH, I NEED IT EVER SO MUCH.

PRECIOUS JESUS PLEASE TAKE CARE. I AM DESPERATE FOR YOUR GRACE AND I LONG TO SEE YOU FACE TO FACE.

PRECIOUS JESUS PLEASE TAKE CARE. I AM DESPERATE FOR YOUR EMBRACE AS I JOURNEY FROM PLACE TO PLACE.

PRECIOUS JESUS PLEASE TAKE CARE. I AM DESPERATE FOR YOUR HOLY POWER, I NEED IT EACH AND EVERY HOUR.

PRECIOUS JESUS PLEASE TAKE CARE OF ME I PRAY. I DO NOT KNOW WHO ELSE I CAN DEPEND ON. PRECIOUS JESUS I WILL MAKE YOU MY HIDING PLACE AND MY COMFORT ZONE. I NEED YOU PRECIOUS JESUS EACH AND EVERY DAY, PLEASE HEAR ME AS I PLUG INTO YOUR HOLY POWER. AMEN AND AMEN.

I REFUSE

I REFUSE TO SAY MY LIFE IS TOUGH PRECIOUS JESUS; BECAUSE IN YOU I HAVE MORE THAN ENOUGH PRECIOUS JESUS.

I REFUSE TO GET DOWN PRECIOUS JESUS; BECAUSE OF YOU I WILL ONE DAY WEAR A GOLDEN CROWN PRECIOUS JESUS.

I REFUSE TO COMPLAIN PRECIOUS JESUS; BECAUSE WITH YOU I WILL ONE DAY REIGN PRECIOUS JESUS.

I REFUSE TO LIVE IN FEAR PRECIOUS JESUS; BECAUSE I KNOW HOW MUCH YOU CARE PRECIOUS JESUS.

I REFUSE TO GIVE UP PRECIOUS JESUS; BECAUSE WITH YOU I WILL ONE DAY BE LIFTED UP PRECIOUS JESUS.

I REFUSE TO LIVE IN DOUBT PRECIOUS JESUS; BECAUSE YOU HAVE SHOWN ME WHAT LIFE IS ALL ABOUT PRECIOUS JESUS.

I REFUSE TO BE IN NEED PRECIOUS JESUS; BECAUSE YOU ARE MY PRECIOUS REDEEMER INDEED PRECIOUS JESUS.

PRECIOUS JESUS ALL I HAVE NEEDED, THINE HANDS HAVE PROVIDED. GREAT INDEED IS THY FAITHFULNESS PRECIOUS LORD JESUS. I SAY THIS WITH UNWAVERING CONFIDENCE IN YOUR PRECIOUS HOLY SWEET NAME JESUS. AMEN AND AMEN.

I AM NOT BEGGING PRECIOUS JESUS, I AM ASKING YOU

I AM NOT BEGGING PRECIOUS JESUS, I AM ASKING YOU TO BLESS ME INDEED SO I CAN SPREAD YOUR ETERNAL SEED.

I AM NOT BEGGING PRECIOUS JESUS, I AM ASKING YOU TO SHOW ME YOUR LOVE SO TRUE SO I CAN BE FAITHFUL ONLY TO YOU.

I AM NOT BEGGING PRECIOUS JESUS, I AM ASKING YOU TO SET MY SPIRIT FREE SO I CAN LIVE ONLY FOR THEE.

I AM NOT BEGGING PRECIOUS JESUS, I AM ASKING YOU TO SHOWER ME WITH YOUR GRACE AS I LOOK INTO YOUR ETERNAL FACE.

I AM NOT BEGGING PRECIOUS JESUS, I AM ASKING YOU TO COMFORT ME IN YOUR ARMS AND COVER ME WITH YOUR CHARMS.

I AM NOT BEGGING PRECIOUS JESUS, I AM ASKING YOU TO DIRECT MY DAILY PATH AS YOU STEER ME FROM YOUR WRATH.

I AM NOT BEGGING PRECIOUS JESUS, I AM ASKING YOU TO LOVE ME SO TRUE SO I COULD NEVER DEPART FROM YOU.

I THANK YOU PRECIOUS JESUS THAT WE/I DO NOT HAVE TO BEG FOR YOUR LOVING KINDNESS AND YOUR TENDER MERCIES. YOU HAVE SPOKEN JESUS AND ORDERED US TO ASK OUR HEAVENLY FATHER IN YOUR NAME AND OUR REQUEST SHALL BE GRANTED. I THANK YOU PRECIOUS JESUS. AMEN AND AMEN.

SO MUCH MORE PRECIOUS JESUS

THE LIFE I LIVE IS BECAUSE OF THE LOVE YOU GIVE AND SO MUCH MORE PRECIOUS JESUS.

AS I WALK ALONG THE WAY AND I HAVE NO WORDS TO SAY, YOU SATISFY ME TODAY AND SO MUCH MORE PRECIOUS JESUS.

THE BURDEN THAT I BARE IS NO MATCH FOR HOW MUCH YOU CARE AND MUCH MORE PRECIOUS JESUS.

AS I LOOK UPON YOU FACE, I BEHOLD YOUR AMAZING GRACE AND SO MUCH MORE PRECIOUS JESUS.

THE BLESSINGS THAT YOU GIVE IS ENOUGH FOR THE LIFE THAT I LIVE AND SO MUCH MORE PRECIOUS JESUS.

AS I WORSHIP YOU TODAY YOU GIVE ME MORE EACH AND EVERYDAY AND SO MUCH MORE PRECIOUS JESUS.

THE SAVIOUR THAT YOU ARE HAS TAKEN AWAY ALL OF MY SCARS AND SO MUCH MORE PRECIOUS JESUS.

I THANK YOU PRECIOUS JESUS FOR DOING SO MUCH MORE THAN I CAN FATHOM. I APPRECIATE YOU PRECIOUS JESUS AND ALL THAT YOU DO. I GIVE MY LOVE TO YOU JESUS AND MY GRATITUDE TOO. AMEN AND AMEN.

MY SPIRIT HUNGERS FOR YOU PRECIOUS JESUS

MY SPIRIT HUNGERS FOR YOU PRECIOUS JESUS MORE THAN WORDS COULD SAY. MY SPIRIT HUNGERS FOR YOU PRECIOUS JESUS, PLEASE SATISFY MY YEARNING TODAY.

MY SPIRIT HUNGERS FOR YOU PRECIOUS JESUS, I AM DESPERATE TO HEAR YOUR VOICE. MY SPIRIT HUNGERS FOR YOU PRECIOUS JESUS, I AM LONGING TO MAKE YOU MY CHOICE.

MY SPIRIT HUNGERS FOR YOU PRECIOUS JESUS AS I AWAKE IN THE EARLY MORNING. MY SPIRIT HUNGERS FOR YOU PRECIOUS JESUS, I LONG FOR YOUR GLORIOUS ADORNING.

MY SPIRIT HUNGERS FOR YOU PRECIOUS JESUS, I HUNGER FOR YOU AT NOON. MY SPIRIT HUNGERS FOR YOU PRECIOUS JESUS, PLEASE SATISFY THIS HUNGER SOON.

MY SPIRIT HUNGERS FOR YOU PRECIOUS JESUS, I HUNGER FOR YOU AT NIGHT. MY SPIRIT HUNGERS FOR YOU PRECIOUS JESUS, PLEASE SATISFY ME WITH YOUR ETERNAL MIGHT.

MY SPIRIT HUNGERS FOR YOU PRECIOUS JESUS, EACH AND EVERY WAKING HOUR. MY SPIRIT HUNGERS FOR YOU PRECIOUS JESUS, PLEASE BLESS ME WITH YOUR EVERLASTING POWER.

MY SPIRIT HUNGERS FOR YOU PRECIOUS JESUS, I NEED YOU TO FILL MY SOUL. MY SPIRIT HUNGERS FOR YOU PRECIOUS JESUS, PLEASE FILL ME AND MAKE ME WHOLE.

PRECIOUS JESUS I AM HUNGRY FOR YOU. PLEASE HELP ME AND GUIDE ME TO THE THINGS THAT ARE PLEASING ONLY TO YOU. I ASK THIS IN YOUR PRECIOUS HOLY NAME JESUS. AMEN AND AMEN.

I CAN NOT WIN WITHOUT YOU PRECIOUS JESUS

I CAN NOT WIN WITHOUT YOU PRECIOUS JESUS BY MY SIDE. PLEASE HELP ME AND LEAD ME AND BE MY GUIDE.

I CAN NOT WIN WITHOUT YOU PRECIOUS JESUS BY MY SIDE. PLEASE HOLD ME AND MOULD ME AND IN YOUR SHADOW I WILL HIDE.

I CAN NOT WIN WITHOUT YOU PRECIOUS JESUS IN MY HEART. PLEASE RESIDE THERE AND NEVER YOU DARE DEPART.

I CAN NOT WIN WITHOUT YOU PRECIOUS JESUS IN MY HEART. PLEASE SHOW ME YOUR MERCY AND YOUR GRACE RIGHT FROM THE START.

I CAN NOT WIN WITHOUT YOU PRECIOUS JESUS IN MY MIND. PLEASE HELP ME TO KNOW THAT YOU ARE ONE OF A KIND.

I CAN NOT WIN WITHOUT YOU PRECIOUS JESUS IN MY MIND. PLEASE RELEASE YOUR SPIRIT AND MAKE ME UNWIND.

I CAN NOT WIN WITHOUT YOU PRECIOUS JESUS SHOWING ME THE WAY. PLEASE HELP ME FROM YOU TO NEVER SWAY.

I THANK YOU PRECIOUS JESUS THAT YOU ARE ALWAYS NEAR AND I KNOW HOW MUCH YOU REALLY CARE. WITHOUT YOU PRECIOUS JESUS I CAN NOT EXIST, I WILL PUT MY TRUST IN YOU AND THIS WORLD RESIST. I PRAY THIS IN YOUR MOST HOLY NAME PRECIOUS JESUS. AMEN AND AMEN.

MAKE ME RIGHT IN YOU PRECIOUS JESUS

MAKE ME RIGHT IN YOU PRECIOUS JESUS. PLEASE MAKE THE WORDS THAT I SAY REFLECT YOU IN THE RIGHT WAY.

MAKE ME RIGHT IN YOU PRECIOUS JESUS. PLEASE ALLOW ME TO ABIDE WITH YOU STILL, WHILE I ACCOMPLISH THY WILL.

MAKE ME RIGHT IN YOU PRECIOUS JESUS. PLEASE DIRECT MY WAY WHILE I LIVE WITH YOU DAY BY DAY.

MAKE ME RIGHT IN YOU PRECIOUS JESUS. PLEASE PLACE WITHIN MY HEART YOUR DESIRE TO NEVER DEPART.

MAKE ME RIGHT IN YOU PRECIOUS JESUS. PLEASE GIVE ME YOUR PIECE OF MIND AND MAKE ME ONE OF YOUR KIND.

MAKE ME RIGHT IN YOU PRECIOUS JESUS. PLEASE ALLOW YOUR WILL TO BE ACCOMPLISHED IN ME STILL.

MAKE ME RIGHT IN YOU PRECIOUS JESUS. PLEASE SHOW ME YOUR LOVE AND LET YOUR HOLY SPIRIT REST UPON ME LIKE A DOVE.

PRECIOUS JESUS, I LONG TO BE RIGHT WITH YOU AND I LONG TO HEAR FROM YOU. PRECIOUS JESUS PLEASE MAKE RIGHT WITH THEE SO I CAN BE SET FREE. I ASK THIS IN YOUR NAME PRECIOUS JESUS. AMEN AND AMEN.

HELP ME TO THINK ABOUT YOU PRECIOUS JESUS

HELP ME TO THINK ABOUT YOU PRECIOUS JESUS AND ALL THE GREAT THINGS THAT YOU DO AND I WILL FOREVER BE GRATEFUL ONTO YOU.

HELP ME TO THINK ABOUT YOU PRECIOUS JESUS AND THE BLESSINGS THAT YOU GIVE AND THE LIFE THAT I NOW LIVE.

HELP ME TO THINK ABOUT YOU PRECIOUS JESUS AND THE GRACE YOU BESTOW WHICH HAS ALLOWED ME TO GROW.

HELP ME TO THINK ABOUT YOU PRECIOUS JESUS AND THE MERCIES THAT YOU GIVE WHICH HAS ALLOWED ME THE PRECIOUS LIFE THAT I LIVE.

HELP ME TO THINK ABOUT YOU PRECIOUS JESUS AND YOUR EVERLASTING POWER SHOWN TO ME EACH AND EVERY HOUR.

HELP ME TO THINK ABOUT YOU PRECIOUS JESUS AND YOUR EVERLASTING GLORY AND I WILL TELL OF YOUR UNENDING STORY.

HELP ME TO THINK ABOUT YOU PRECIOUS JESUS AND YOUR ETERNAL LOVE THAT HAS TRANSFORMED ME FROM HEAVEN ABOVE.

PRECIOUS JESUS, I AM THANKFUL FOR YOUR GRATEFULNESS, YOUR BLESSINGS, YOUR GRACE, YOUR MERCIES, YOUR POWER, YOUR GLORY AND YOUR ETERNAL LOVE. I AM THANKFUL FOR ALL THAT YOU DO AND THE LOVE YOU GIVE TO ME TOO. I CLAIM THIS IN YOUR MIGHTY NAME SWEET JESUS. AMEN AND AMEN.

PRECIOUS JESUS PLEASE FORGIVE ME FOR INSULTING YOU

PRECIOUS JESUS PLEASE FORGIVE ME FOR INSULTING YOU AND FOR MY LIMITED THOUGHT I HAVE OF YOU.

PRECIOUS JESUS PLEASE FORGIVE ME FOR INSULTING YOU AND FOR THE DOUBT THAT IS WITHIN MY HEART TOWARDS YOU.

PRECIOUS JESUS PLEASE FORGIVE ME FOR INSULTING YOU AND FOR DEPENDING ON MANKIND INSTEAD OF YOU.

PRECIOUS JESUS PLEASE FORGIVE ME FOR INSULTING YOU AND FOR MY DESPERATION INSTEAD OF ASKING OF YOU.

PRECIOUS JESUS PLEASE FORGIVE ME FOR INSULTING YOU AND FOR NOT COUNTING MY BLESSINGS THAT CAME FROM YOU.

PRECIOUS JESUS PLEASE FORGIVE ME FOR INSULTING YOU AND FOR MY SHORTSIGHTEDNESS I HAVE TOWARDS YOU.

PRECIOUS JESUS PLEASE FORGIVE ME FOR INSULTING YOU BECAUSE THERE IS NO BETTER SHEPHERD I HAVE BESIDES YOU.

I THANK YOU PRECIOUS JESUS THAT YOU WILL NEVER DISAPPOINT ME. I THANK YOU THAT LIFE LESSONS HAVE BROUGHT ME TO DEPEND SOLEY ON YOU. I THANK YOU FOR BLESSING ME PRECIOUS HEAVENLY FATHER. I THANK YOU FOR COMFORTING ME PRECIOUS HOLY SPIRIT. I PRAY THIS IN THE PRECIOUS MIGHTY NAME OF JESUS. AMEN AND AMEN.

I THANK YOU PRECIOUS JESUS

I THANK YOU PRECIOUS JESUS FOR YOUR LIFE, YOU GIVE ME STRENGTH TO CARRY ON THIS FIGHT.

I THANK YOU PRECIOUS JESUS FOR YOUR HEALTH, YOU MAKE ME WHOLE AND GRANT ME WEALTH.

I THANK YOU PRECIOUS JESUS FOR YOUR LOVE, YOU SHOWER ME WITH YOUR BLESSINGS FROM ABOVE.

I THANK YOU PRECIOUS JESUS FOR YOUR BLESSINGS, YOU TEACH ME EVERYDAY ABOUT YOUR LIFE LESSONS.

I THANK YOU PRECIOUS JESUS FOR YOUR POWER, YOU PROVE IT TO ME EACH AND EVERY HOUR.

I THANK YOU PRECIOUS JESUS FOR TODAY, FOR THIS THE ETERNAL PRICE YOU DID PAY.

I THANK YOU PRECIOUS JESUS FOR TOMORROW, FOR I KNOW YOU WILL PROTECT ME FROM HARM AND SORROW.

PRECIOUS HOLY SPIRIT PLEASE TEACH ME HOW TO GIVE THANKS EACH AND EVERY DAY TO MY HEAVENLY AND MY PRECIOUS SAVIOUR JESUS. I ASK THIS IN THE MIGHTY AND PRECIOUS NAME OF JESUS. AMEN AND AMEN.

PRECIOUS JESUS WHY CAN'T WE SEE

PRECIOUS JESUS WHY CAN'T WE SEE HOW MUCH YOU CARE AND HOW MUCH YOU ARE WILLING TO SHARE.

PRECIOUS JESUS WHY CAN'T WE SEE THAT THE PATH YOU MAKE IS THE ONE WE SHOULD TAKE.

PRECIOUS JESUS WHY CAN'T WE SEE THAT YOUR RADIANT FACE REFLECTS YOUR AMAZING GRACE.

PRECIOUS JESUS WHY CAN'T WE SEE THAT THE MERCIES YOU BESTOW IS THERE TO MAKE US GROW.

PRECIOUS JESUS WHY CAN'T WE SEE THAT THE BLOOD YOU SHED IS THERE TO RAISE US FROM THE DEAD.

PRECIOUS JESUS WHY CAN'T WE SEE THAT YOUR SHEKHINAH GLORY TELLS US OF YOUR WONDERFUL STORY.

PRECIOUS JESUS WHY CAN'T WE SEE THAT THE LOVE YOU GIVE IS SO MANKIND CAN LIVE.

PRECIOUS JESUS TEACH US/ME BY YOUR PRECIOUS HOLY SPIRIT HOW TO SEE YOU AS YOU ARE. TEACH US PRECIOUS HOLY SPIRIT HOW TO SEE OUR HEAVENLY FATHER THROUGH THE EYES AND HEART BEAT OF JESUS. I ASK THIS IN THE MOST PRECIOUS NAME OF JESUS. AMEN AND AMEN.

I AM THE LIVING (PRECIOUS JESUS) WATER

PRECIOUS JESUS YOU ARE THE LIVING WATER, THE ONE ALL MANKIND SHOULD BE SEEKING AFTER.

PRECIOUS JESUS YOU ARE THE LIVING WATER, YOU GIVE LIFE IN THE NOW AND THE HEREAFTER.

PRECIOUS JESUS YOU ARE THE LIVING WATER, ONE TASTE OF YOU AND WE WILL HAVE YOU AS OUR ETERNAL MASTER.

PRECIOUS JESUS YOU ARE THE LIVING WATER, ONE TOUCH BY YOU AND YOU WILL RESCUE US FROM ALL DISASTER.

PRECIOUS JESUS YOU ARE THE LIVING WATER, ONE WORD FROM YOU WILL APPROVE US TO BE YOUR SON AND DAUGHTER.

PRECIOUS JESUS YOU ARE THE LIVING WATER, ONE KISS FROM YOU WILL SATISFY US TODAY AND FOREVER-AFTER.

PRECIOUS JESUS YOU ARE THE LIVING WATER, ONE DRINK OF YOU WILL QUENCH OUR THIRST AND GRANT US EVERLASTING LAUGHTER.

PRECIOUS JESUS YOU SAID IN JOHN 4:10 "JESUS ANSWERED AND SAID TO HER, IF YOU KNEW THE GIFT OF GOD AND WHO IS SAYING TO YOU, GIVE ME A DRINK, YOU WOULD HAVE ASKED HIM AND HE WOULD HAVE GIVEN YOU LIVING WATER." HEAVENLY FATHER I AM ASKING IN THE PRECIOUS NAME OF JESUS FOR YOUR LIVING WATER. IN JESUS PRECIOUS NAME I ASK. AMEN AND AMEN.

THE WORLD NEEDS TO KNOW YOU PRECIOUS LORD JESUS

EVERY MAN, EVERY WOMAN AND EVERY CHILD. THE WORLD NEEDS TO KNOW HOW LOVING, HOW GENTLE AND HOW MILD YOU ARE, PRECIOUS LORD JESUS.

EVERY SECOND, EVERY MINUTE AND EVERY HOUR. THE WORLD NEEDS TO KNOW OF YOUR UNLIMITED POWER, PRECIOUS LORD JESUS.

EVERY DAY, EVERY MONTH AND EVERY YEAR. THE WORLD NEEDS TO KNOW HOW MUCH YOU CARE, PRECIOUS LORD JESUS.

EVERY BREATH, EVERY STEP AND EVERY THOUGHT. THE WORLD NEEDS TO KNOW HOW GREAT THOU ART, PRECIOUS LORD JESUS.

EVERY TURNING, EVERY BURNING AND EVERY YEARNING. THE WORLD NEEDS TO KNOW YOU SOON WILL BE RETURNING, PRECIOUS LORD JESUS.

EVERY LETTER, EVERY WORD AND EVERY PHRASE. THE WORLD NEEDS TO GIVE YOU ALL OF ITS' PRAISE, PRECIOUS LORD JESUS.

EVERY BROOK, EVERY STREAM AND EVERY RIVER. THE WORLD NEEDS TO KNOW YOU ARE THE ONLY ONE THAT CAN DELIVER, PRECIOUS LORD JESUS.

EVERY MOMENT WE LIVE, WE HAVE THANKS TO GIVE AND IT'S BECAUSE OF YOU PRECIOUS JESUS. AMEN AND AMEN.

I DON'T KNOW WHAT TO DO
PRECIOUS LORD JESUS

I AM TRYING PRECIOUS JESUS, I DON'T KNOW WHAT TO DO.
I AM CRYING PRECIOUS JESUS, PLEASE HELP ME TO RETURN ONLY TO YOU.

I AM TRYING PRECIOUS JESUS, I DON'T KNOW WHAT TO SAY.
I AM CRYING PRECIOUS JESUS, PLEASE HELP ME TO FIND MY WAY.

I AM TRYING PRECIOUS JESUS, I DON'T KNOW WHAT LIFE HAS IN STORE
FOR ME.
I AM CRYING PRECIOUS JESUS, PLEASE HELP MY BLIND EYES TO SEE.

I AM TRYING PRECIOUS JESUS, I DON'T KNOW WHAT HAPPENED TO MY
HEART.
I AM CRYING PRECIOUS JESUS, PLEASE HELP ME TO MAKE A BRAND NEW
START.

I AM TRYING PRECIOUS JESUS, I DON'T KNOW WHAT I CAN GIVE.
I AM CRYING PRECIOUS JESUS, PLEASE HELP ME LOVE YOU AS LONG AS
I LIVE.

I AM TRYING PRECIOUS JESUS, I DON'T KNOW WHAT STEPS TO TAKE.
I AM CRYING PRECIOUS JESUS, PLEASE HELP ME TO AVOID ANOTHER
MISTAKE.

I AM TRYING PRECIOUS JESUS, I DON'T KNOW IF I SHOULD CARE.
I AM CRYING PRECIOUS JESUS, PLEASE HELP ME TO UNLOAD WHAT I
CANNOT BARE.

I AM CALLING ON YOU PRECIOUS HOLY FATHER, I AM CALLING ON YOU
PRECIOUS LORD JESUS AND CALLING ON YOU PRECIOUS HOLY SPIRIT.
PLEASE HELP ME I PRAY IN JESUS MOST PRECIOUS NAME I ASK THIS.
AMEN AND AMEN.

THANK YOU JESUS FOR BLESSING ME

THANK YOU JESUS FOR BLESSING ME. THANK YOU JESUS FOR MAKING ME THE BEST I CAN BE.

THANK YOU JESUS FOR BLESSING ME. THANK YOU JESUS FOR ALLOWING ME TO SEE ALL WHAT LIFE HAS IN STORE FOR ME.

THANK YOU JESUS FOR BLESSING ME. THANK YOU JESUS FOR GIVING ME LIFE AND HEALTH FOR ALL TO SEE.

THANK YOU JESUS FOR BLESSING ME. THANK YOU JESUS FOR SETTING MY SPIRIT FREE.

THANK YOU JESUS FOR BLESSING ME. THANK YOU JESUS FOR MAKING ME ACCEPTING OF THEE.

THANK YOU JESUS FOR BLESSING ME. THANK YOU JESUS FOR MAKING MY LIFE EASY AS ONE, TWO, THREE.

THANK YOU JESUS FOR BLESSING ME. I WILL THANK YOU LORD JESUS FOR ALL ETERNITY.

I THANK YOU PRECIOUS LORD JESUS FOR ALL THAT YOU HAVE DONE AND WILL CONTINUE TO DO FOR ME. FROM THE BOTTOM OF MY HEART I THANK YOU MY PRECIOUS SAVIOUR. AMEN AND AMEN.

PRECIOUS JESUS KING OF GLORY

PRECIOUS JESUS KING OF GLORY, PLEASE TELL ME OF YOUR WONDERFUL STORY.
PRECIOUS JESUS KING OF GLORY, PLEASE HELP ME NEVER TO WORRY.

PRECIOUS JESUS KING OF GLORY, PLEASE TELL ME OF YOUR REDEMPTION WAY.
PRECIOUS JESUS KING OF GLORY, PLEASE HELP ME NEVER TO GO ASTRAY.

PRECIOUS JESUS KING OF GLORY, PLEASE TELL ME OF YOUR EVERLASTING LOVE.
PRECIOUS JESUS KING OF GLORY, PLEASE HELP ME TO DEPEND FROM THE THINGS ABOVE.

PRECIOUS JESUS KING OF GLORY, PLEASE TELL ME OF YOUR BURNING DESIRE.
PRECIOUS JESUS KING OF GLORY, PLEASE HELP ME TO DO THE THINGS YOU REQUIRE.

PRECIOUS JESUS KING OF GLORY, PLEASE TELL ME OF YOUR MERCY AND GRACE.
PRECIOUS JESUS KING OF GLORY, PLEASE HELP ME TO ENDURE THIS RACE.

PRECIOUS JESUS KING OF GLORY, PLEASE TELL ME OF YOUR ETERNAL PLAN.
PRECIOUS JESUS KING OF GLORY, PLEASE HELP ME, I NEED YOUR HELPING HAND.

PRECIOUS JESUS KING OF GLORY, PLEASE TELL ME HOW MUCH YOU CARE.
PRECIOUS JESUS KING OF GLORY, PLEASE HELP ME TO SEE THAT YOU ARE ALWAYS NEAR.

PRECIOUS JESUS YOU ARE INDEED THE KING OF GLORY. PLEASE HELP ME JUST TO TASTE AND SEE THAT YOU ARE GOOD PRECIOUS LORD JESUS. PLEASE HELP ME TO WORSHIP YOU LIKE I SHOULD. I PRAY THIS IN YOUR MIGHTY NAME PRECIOUS LORD JESUS. AMEN AND AMEN.

JUST LOVE

IF WE COULD LOVE EACH OTHER WITH AN OPEN MIND. OH WHAT JOY WOULD COME TO ALL MANKIND.

IF WE COULD BLESS EACH OTHER WITH A GIFT. OH WHAT JOY WOULD COME TO THE LIFE WE LIFT.

IF WE COULD TEACH EACH OTHER TO BE TRUE. OH WHAT JOY THERE WOULD BE FOR ME AND FOR YOU.

IF WE COULD TEACH EACH OTHER TO BE KIND. OH WHAT JOY WOULD BE YOURS AND MINE.

IF WE COULD TEACH EACH OTHER TO DO THEIR BEST. OH WHAT JOY WOULD BE YOURS TO DIGEST.

IF WE COULD TEACH EACH OTHER TO HAVE A HEART. OH WHAT JOY WOULD BE YOURS TO IMPART.

IF WE COULD TEACH EACH OTHER TO GIVE A SMILE. OH WHAT JOY WOULD BE YOURS MILE AFTER MILE.

PLEASE TEACH ME HOW TO LOVE LIKE YOU LOVE PRECIOUS LORD JESUS. "GREATER LOVE HAS NO ONE THAN THIS, TO LAY DOWN ONE'S LIFE FOR HIS FRIENDS". JOHN 15:13

IN TIME OF NEED, IN TIME OF TROUBLES, PRAYER IS THE ANSWER! IN OUR EARNESTNESS JESUS HEARS AND RESPONDS TO OUR PLEA. GIVE HIM YOUR ALL AND HE WILL ANSWER YOUR BECKONING CALL.

SO MY FRIENDS, WON'T YOU CALL UPON THE PRECIOUS NAME OF JESUS TODAY.

ABOUT THE AUTHOR

THE AUTHOR IS A RETIRED POLICE OFFICER WHO HAS SEEN A GREAT DEAL OF STRUGGLES FROM ALL WALKS OF LIFE. THIS HAS DRIVEN HIM TO CRY OUT TO GOD IN THE PRECIOUS NAME OF JESUS AND IN DOING SO HAS INSPIRED HIM TO WRITE THESE INSPIRATIONAL REVELATIONS.

Printed in the United States
By Bookmasters